The Little Seashore Activity Book

by Anna Pomaska

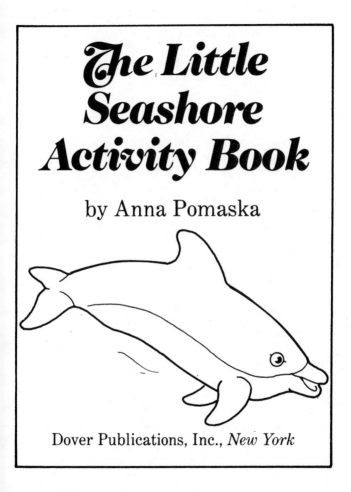

Dover Publications, Inc., *New York*

Published in Canada by General Publishing Company, Ltd., 30 Lesmill Road, Don Mills, Toronto, Ontario.
Published in the United Kingdom by Constable and Company, Ltd.

The Little Seashore Activity Book is a new work, first published by Dover Publications, Inc., in 1988.

International Standard Book Number: 0-486-25608-1

Manufactured in the United States of America
Dover Publications, Inc., 31 East 2nd Street, Mineola, N.Y. 11501

Note

Whether you do these puzzles right at the seashore, on the way there, on the way back, or even at home, they are sure to entertain you. There are crossword puzzles, hidden pictures, follow-the-dots games, what's-wrong-with-this-picture games, hidden words, mazes, counting games, and nature identification pages to be colored. (In fact, you can color any of the pages.) For all of the puzzles and activities that call for an answer, you will find the solutions in the section that begins on page 56. Now the beach will be even more fun than it ever was!

Judy and Jany are having so much fun making a sand castle, they don't see the 2 fish and 3 shells hidden around them. Can you find them?

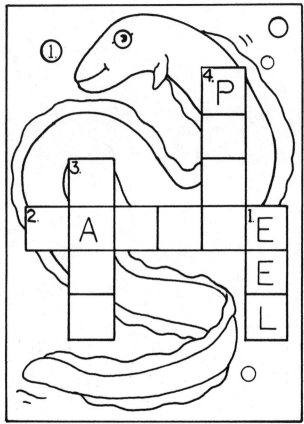

To do this crossword puzzle, spell out the names of the things shown on the opposite page. The numbers next to the pictures tell you where the names belong in the puzzle.

8

SEA GULL

Sea gulls are very beautiful to watch when they fly.
Color this gull like the ones you see at the shore.

10

SEA GULL

Sea gulls will eat almost anything they find in the water or on shore. Most gulls are gray or white, with yellow bill and legs.

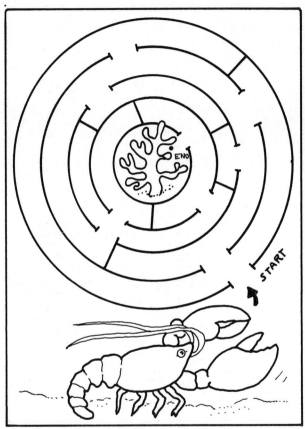

Larry Lobster would like to eat the seaweed. Help him find the right way to reach it.

This picture of Susan on the beach has 4 things that are out of place. Can you see them?

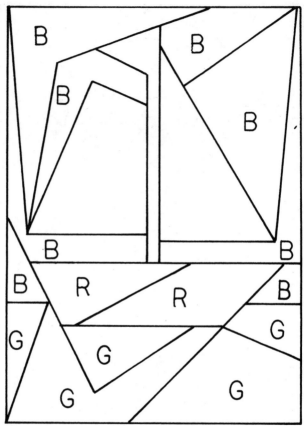

You will make a hidden picture appear if you color all the shapes marked "G" green, all the "B" shapes blue and the two "R" shapes red.

14

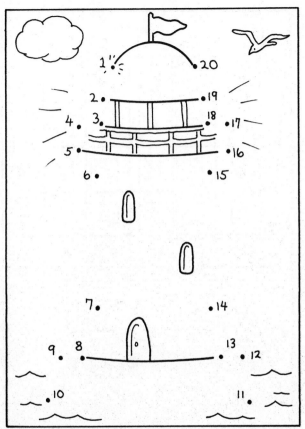

Connect the dots 1 through 20 to see what is shining so brightly.

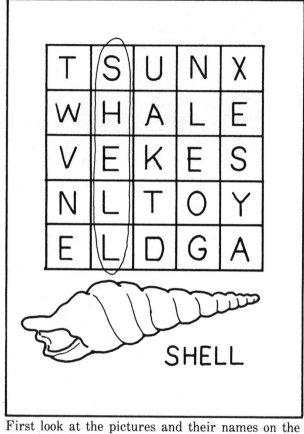

T	S	U	N	X
W	H	A	L	E
V	E	K	E	S
N	L	T	O	Y
E	L	D	G	A

SHELL

First look at the pictures and their names on the opposite page. Then find those names hidden in the box above and circle them, just the way the word "shell" is circled.

SUN

WHALE

TOY

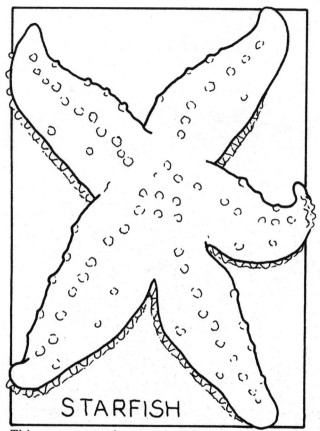

STARFISH

This sea creature's name is easy to remember—it looks like a star! Starfish may be tan or other colors.

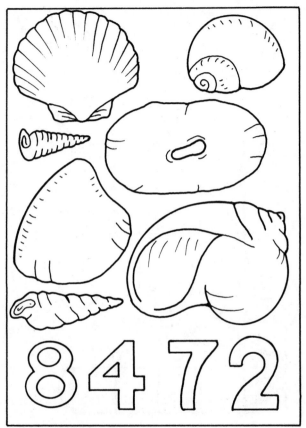

How many shiny shells are here? Count them and circle the right number.

To do this crossword puzzle, spell out the names of the things shown on the opposite page. The numbers next to the pictures tell you where the names belong in the puzzle.

20

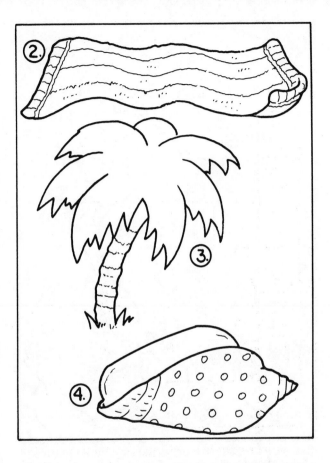

2.

3.

4.

21

Can you find the 4 hidden fishes in this picture of
Molly Mermaid?

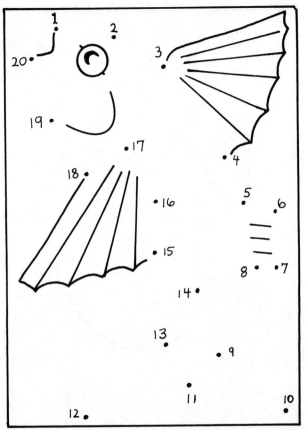

Here's somebody who can swim and fly! Connect the dots 1 through 20 to see who it is.

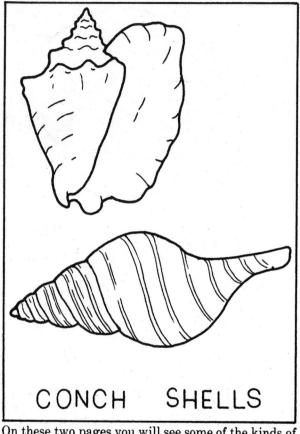

CONCH SHELLS

On these two pages you will see some of the kinds of shells you may find when you visit the seashore.

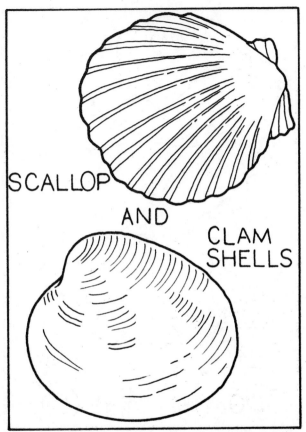

SCALLOP

AND

CLAM
SHELLS

Clam shells are usually gray; and scallop shells,
yellow. Conch shells may be of very different colors.

How many spunky seals are here? Count them and circle the right number.

In this picture of Janet swimming underwater, 4 things are out of place. Can you find them?

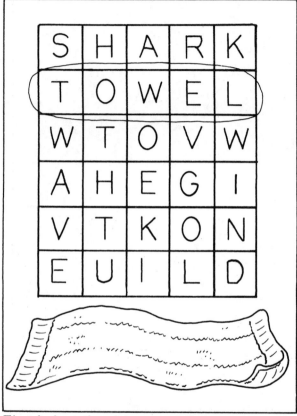

S	H	A	R	K
T	O	W	E	L
W	T	O	V	W
A	H	E	G	I
V	T	K	O	N
E	U	I	L	D

First look at the pictures and their names on the opposite page. Then find those names hidden in the box above and circle them, just the way the word "towel" is circled.

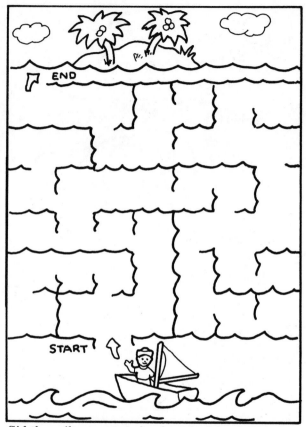

Sid the sailor wants to land on the island. Help him over the sea without crossing any lines.

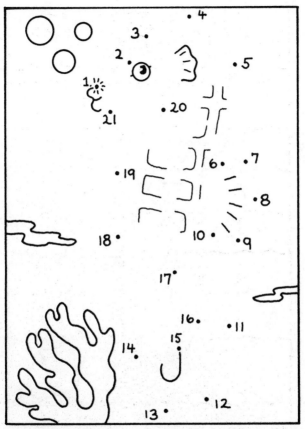

Connect the dots 1 through 21 and make this seashore friend appear.

In this picture of Bobby and Leslie on the beach there are 5 things wrong or out of place. Can you find them?

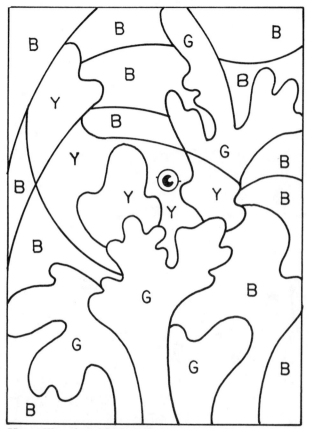

You will make a hidden picture appear if you color all
the shapes marked "B" blue, all the "G" shapes green
and all the "Y" shapes yellow.

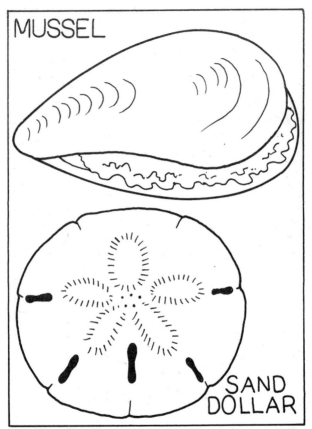

MUSSEL

SAND DOLLAR

Shells protect the creatures that live inside them, like the mussel. Mussel shells are dark blue or brown. Sand dollars can be brown, yellow or purple.

34

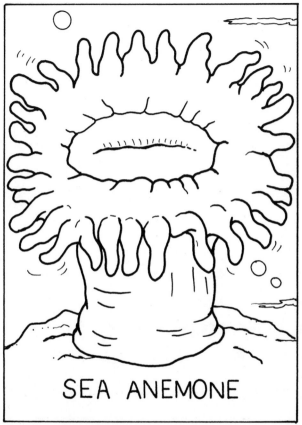

SEA ANEMONE

Sea anemones, which have a big range of bright colors, attach themselves to rocks and catch fish with their waving tentacles.

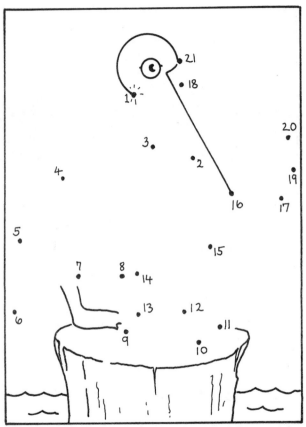

Who is standing here looking at the sea? Connect the dots 1 through 21 to find out.

Three fish that Billy wants to catch are hiding from him. Can you see them?

To do this crossword puzzle, spell out the names of the things shown on the opposite page. The numbers next to the pictures tell you where the names belong in the puzzle.

38

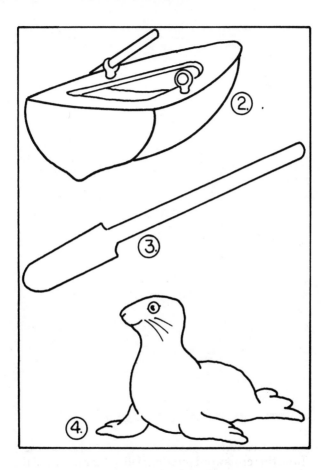

How many funny fish are here? Count them and circle the right number.

Connie the crab wants to visit her friend Sammy the sea horse, but she has forgotten the way. Please help her!

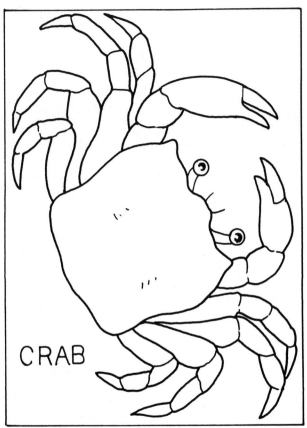

CRAB

The crab has an outer covering of hard material that is like a shell. There are crabs of many different colors.

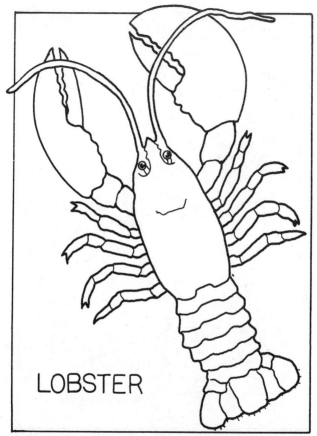

LOBSTER

Lobsters have two main claws, of which one is usually larger than the other. American lobsters are blackish green on top and reddish below.

Danny the diver hopes to find the sunken treasure.
Help him get there without crossing any lines.

In this picture of Tommy exploring under the sea there are 4 things out of place. Can you find them?

45

SEA URCHIN

The sea urchin catches its food with its tentacles. Red, purple and green are some of the colors of different sea urchins.

JELLYFISH

Jellyfish look very graceful floating through the sea. The color varies greatly from one kind to another.

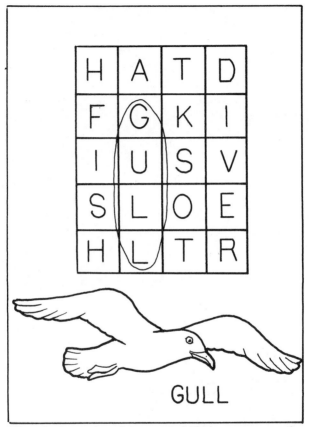

H	A	T	D
F	G	K	I
I	U	S	V
S	L	O	E
H	L	T	R

GULL

First look at the pictures and their names on the opposite page. Then find those names hidden in the box above and circle them, just the way the word "gull" is circled.

FISH

DIVER

HAT

49

Mary is very excited about what she has made.
Connect the dots 1 through 21 to see her creation.

In this sailboat that Sally is steering, 7 letters of the alphabet are hidden: N, Y, A, L, S, d and i. Can you find them?

How many dandy dolphins are here? Count them and circle the right number.

SEAWEED

Seaweed is a type of plant that lives in the sea. It can be green, brown or red.

In this picture of Peter playing on the beach with his watering can there are 5 things out of place. Can you find them?

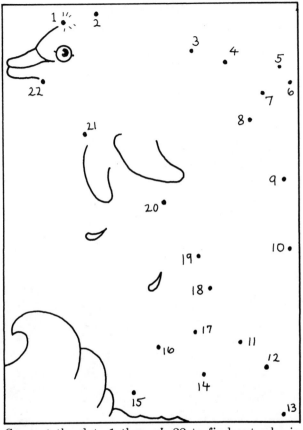

Connect the dots 1 through 22 to find out who is smiling so happily.

Solutions

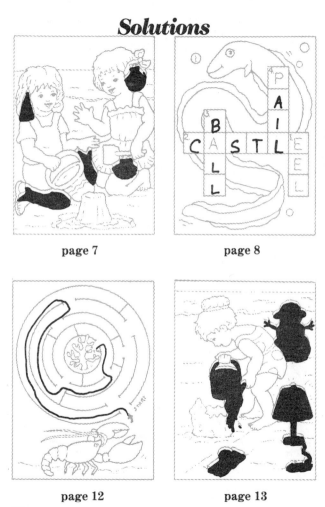

page 7

page 8

page 12

page 13

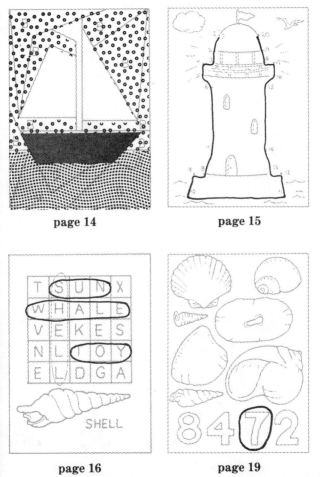

page 14

page 15

page 16

page 19

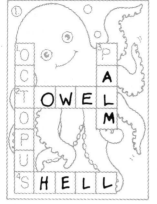

page 20

page 22

page 23

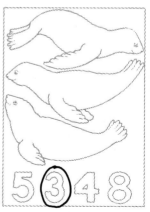

page 26

page 27

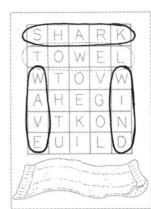

page 28

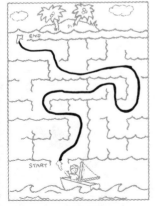

page 30

page 31

page 32

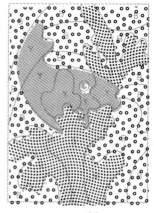

page 33

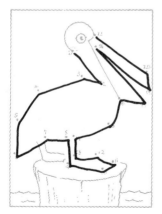

page 36

page 37

page 38

page 40

page 41

page 44

page 45

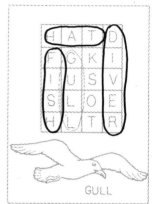

page 48

page 50

page 51

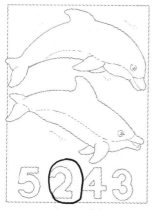

page 52

page 54

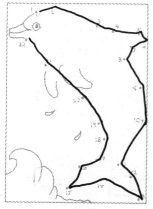

page 55